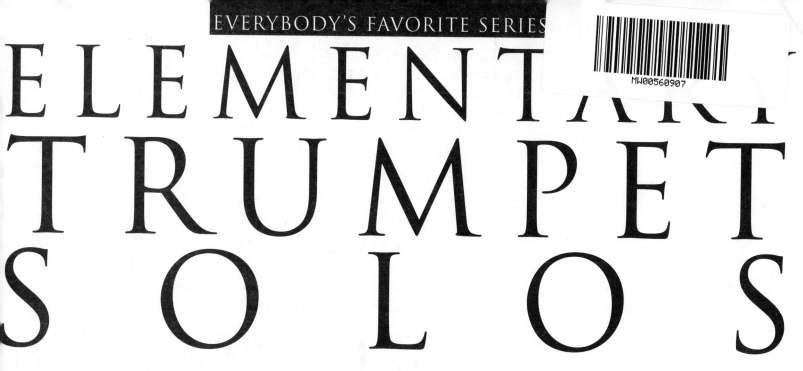

ELEMENTARY TRUMPET SOLOS

Everybody's Favorite Series

MW00560907

Edited by Jay Arnold.
Contains a wide variety of material ranging from the works of the
classical composers to lighter melodies and songs. A most useful
collection for private teachers, schools, and musicians alike.
With piano accompaniment.

ORDER NO. AM 40163
INTERNATIONAL STANDARD BOOK NUMBER: 0.8256.2032.5

EXCLUSIVE DISTRIBUTORS:
MUSIC SALES CORPORATION
257 PARK AVENUE SOUTH, NEW YORK, NY 10010 USA
MUSIC SALES LIMITED
8/9 FRITH STREET, LONDON W1V 5TZ ENGLAND
MUSIC SALES PTY. LIMITED
120 ROTHSCHILD STREET, ROSEBERY, SYDNEY, NSW 2018, AUSTRALIA

PRINTED IN THE UNITED STATES OF AMERICA BY
VICKS LITHOGRAPH AND PRINTING CORPORATION

Amsco Publications
New York/London/Paris/Sydney/Copenhagen/Madrid

Elementary Trumpet Solos

CONTENTS

Elementary Trumpet Solos

CONTENTS BY COMPOSERS

Scenes From Childhood
1. From Foreign Lands

SCHUMANN

2. SOLDIER'S MARCH

3. FIRST GRIEF

4. THE WILD HORSEMAN

5. THE MERRY PEASANT.

ANDANTE CANTABILE
FROM THE QUARTET OP. 11

P.I. TSCHAIKOWSKY

La Golondrina

N. SERRADELL

Carry Me Back To Old Virginny

JAMES BLAND

Made in U.S.A.

Silver Threads Among The Gold

H. P. DANKS

LITTLE ANNIE ROONEY

MICHAEL NOLAN

Du, Du Liegst Mir Im Herzen

GERMAN FOLK SONG

Ah! I Have Sighed To Rest Me

From "Il Trovatore"

VERDI

Come Back To Sorrento

DE CURTIS

Loch Lomond

SCOTCH SONG

Andante con moto

Rose Of Tralee

GLOVER

Valse Andante

Made in U.S.A.

Consolation

MENDELSSOHN

APACHE DANCE

OFFENBACH

Slavonic Dance

DVORAK

On Wings Of Song

MENDELSSOHN

Andante tranquillo

ON WINGS OF SONG (continued)

Norwegian Dance

GRIEG

Largo
from the New World Symphony

ANTON DVORAK

WALTZ

J. BRAHMS, Op 39 No 15

Grazioso

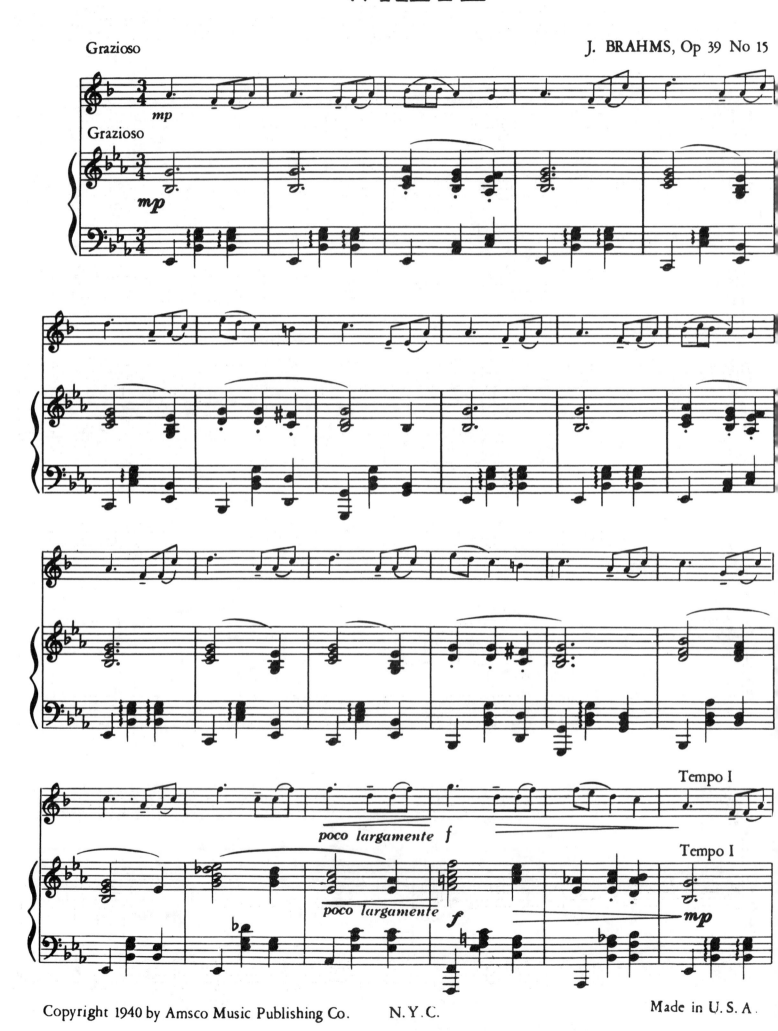

Palm Branches
(Les Rameaux)

J. FAURE

Andante maestoso

Long, Long Ago

Moderato

THOMAS HAYNES BAYLY

Old Oaken Bucket

SAMUEL WOODWORTH

La Cucaracha

POPULAR MEXICAN SONG

Wearing Of The Green

IRISH SONG

Cradle Song

M. HAUSER, Op 11 No 2

DOROTHY
OLD ENGLISH DANCE

SEYMOUR SMITH

La Cinquantaine

GABRIEL · MARIE

Waltz From "Faust"

GOUNOD

WALTZ FROM "FAUST" (continued)

cantabile
mf

Funiculi Funicula

LUIGI DENZA

EVENING STAR
(TANNHAUSER)

WAGNER

A FRANGESA

COSTA

Jeanie With The Light Brown Hair

STEPHEN FOSTER

Beautiful Dreamer

STEPHEN FOSTER

Merry Widow Waltz

D.S. ℅ al Fine

D.S. ℅ al Fine

SCARF DANCE

C. CHAMINADE

Rock of Ages

HASTINGS

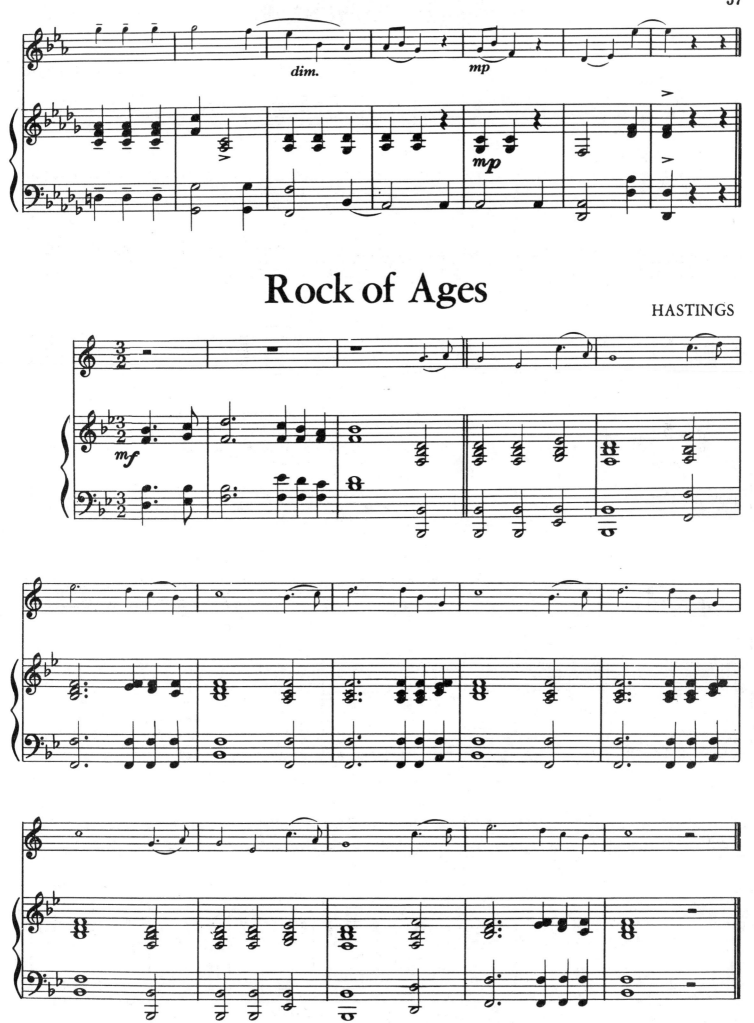

Abide With Me

W. H. MONK

Hark! The Herald Angels Sing

F. MENDELSSOHN

Tango in D

Andantino grazioso

ALBENIZ

A Media Luz

E. DONATO

Gold And Silver
Waltz

LEHAR

GOLD AND SILVER (continued)

Comin' Thru The Rye

ROBERT BURNS

Moderato

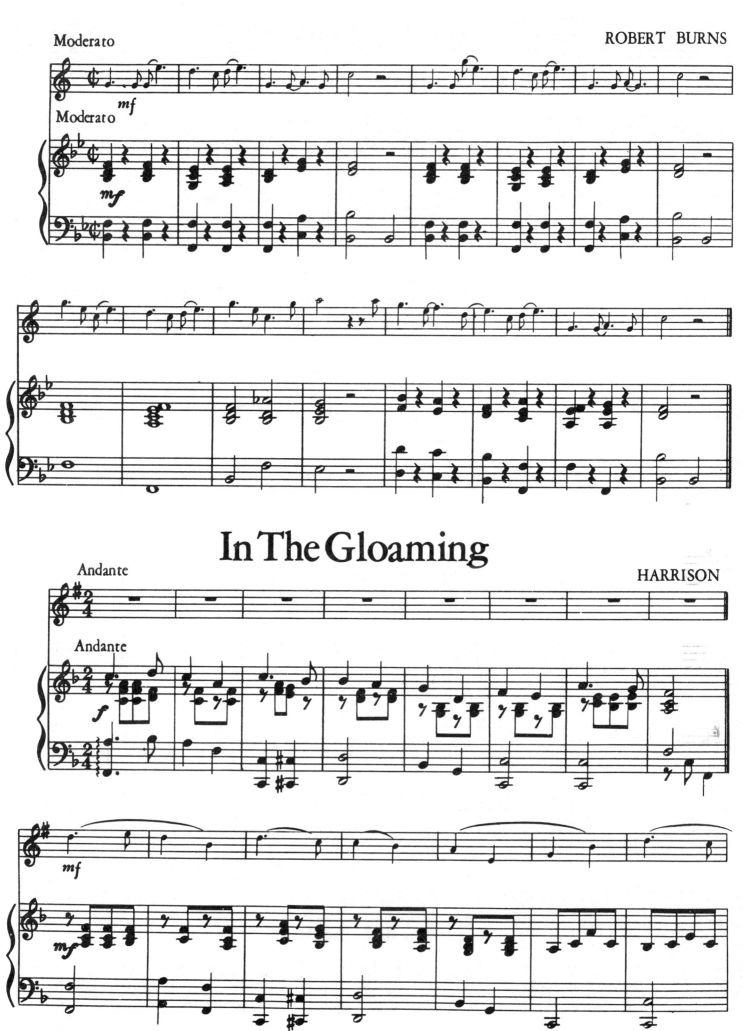

In The Gloaming

HARRISON

Andante

Santa Lucia

NEAPOLITAN SONG

AY, AY, AY

CREOLE SONG

MARYLAND, MY MARYLAND

VILIA
from the MERRY WIDOW

FRANZ LEHAR

LIEBESTRAUM
(Dream of Love)

FRANZ LISZT

Scenes That Are Brightest

Andante cantabile

WALLACE

AMARYLLIS

Allegro moderato

H. GHYS

SWEET AND LOW

BARNBY

Waltz In A Minor

Tempo di Valse

EDVARD GRIEG, Op 12, No. 2

WALTZ IN A MINOR (continued)

WALTZ IN A MINOR (continued)

GRAND MARCH

from
AIDA

G. VERDI

MOMENT MUSICAL

FRANZ SCHUBERT, Op. 94

SOLVEJG'S SONG

EDVARD GRIEG

Flower Song
BLUMENLIED

GUSTAV LANGE

Heavenly Aida

From the Opera "AIDA"

GUISEPPE VERDI

ANDANTINO

E. LEMARE

GOOD NIGHT LADIES

FIFTH NOCTURNE

LEYBACH

Chanson Triste

P. I. TSCHAIKOWSKY, Op 40, No. 2

Home Sweet Home

HENRY BISHOP

Massa's In De Cold, Cold Ground

STEPHEN FOSTER

My Old Kentucky Home

STEPHEN FOSTER

OLD BLACK JOE

STEPHEN FOSTER

LA MARSEILLAISE

DE LISLE

ALOHA OE

QUEEN LILIUOKALANI

YANKEE DOODLE

AMERICAN SONG

Columbia The Gem Of The Ocean

SHAW

The Man On The Flying Trapeze

SERENADE

G. PIERNE

Waves Of The Danube

IVANOVICI

Il Bacio

L. ARDITI

Tales From The Vienna Woods

J. STRAUSS

TALES FROM THE VIENNA WOODS (continued)

Country Gardens

ENGLISH FOLK DANCE

OLD FRENCH SONG

P.I. TSCHAIKOWSKY, Op 39, No.14

The Skaters
WALTZ

E. WALDTEUFEL

THE SKATERS (continued)

Whispering Hope

ALICE HAWTHORNE